NATURE PUZZLES

Bugs and Butterflies

A First Spotter's Activity Book

Written by Catherine Bruzzone
Illustrated by Sarah Dennis

How to use the flashcards:

Cut out and keep the flashcards on the front and back cover flaps. Carry them around in your pocket and write on the back of them when you spot each creature. Some will be harder to spot than others.

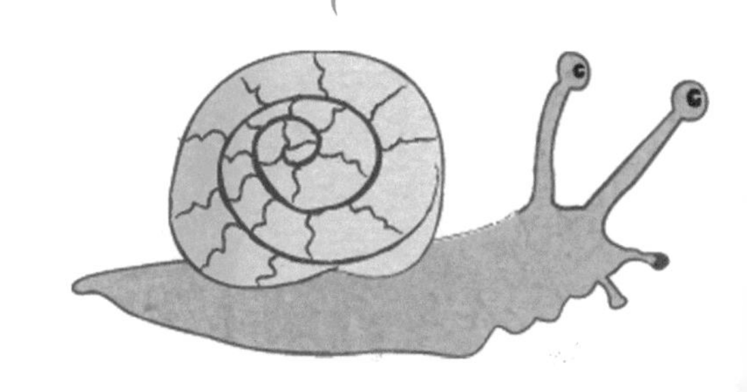

b small publishing
www.bsmall.co.uk

Can you spot 18 different bugs and butterflies in this picture?

Turn the page to find out
more about them...

Honey Bee

Count the bees on their way to the hive.

Did you know?

Bees make **honey**. Bees must visit about two million flowers to make half a kilo of honey.

Wasp

These wasps want to eat the picnic food.
Can you spot 5 differences between the pictures?

Colour in the picnic cloth.

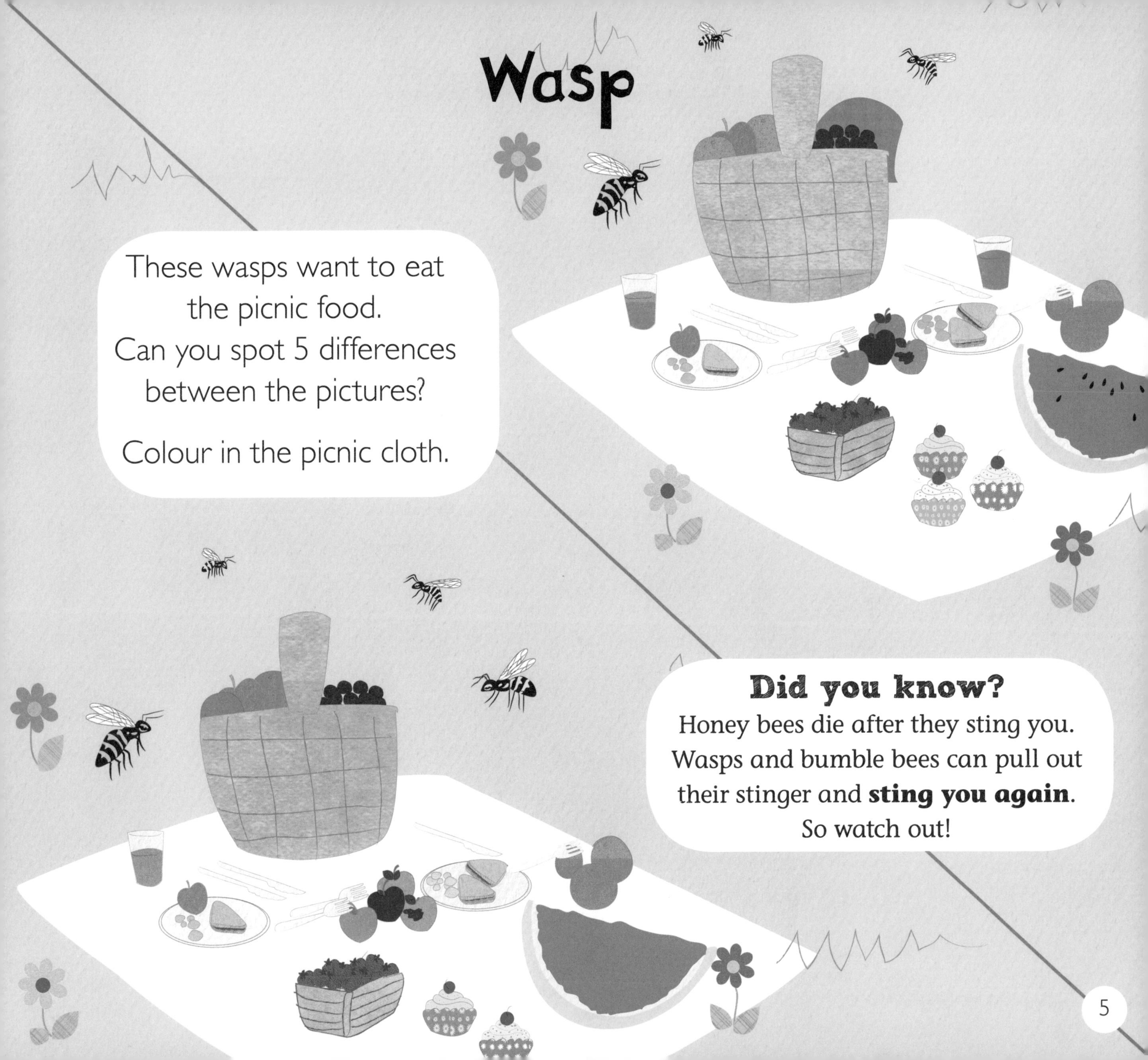

Did you know?

Honey bees die after they sting you. Wasps and bumble bees can pull out their stinger and **sting you again**. So watch out!

Grasshopper

Join the dots and see where this grasshopper has hopped.

Finish colouring in the picture.

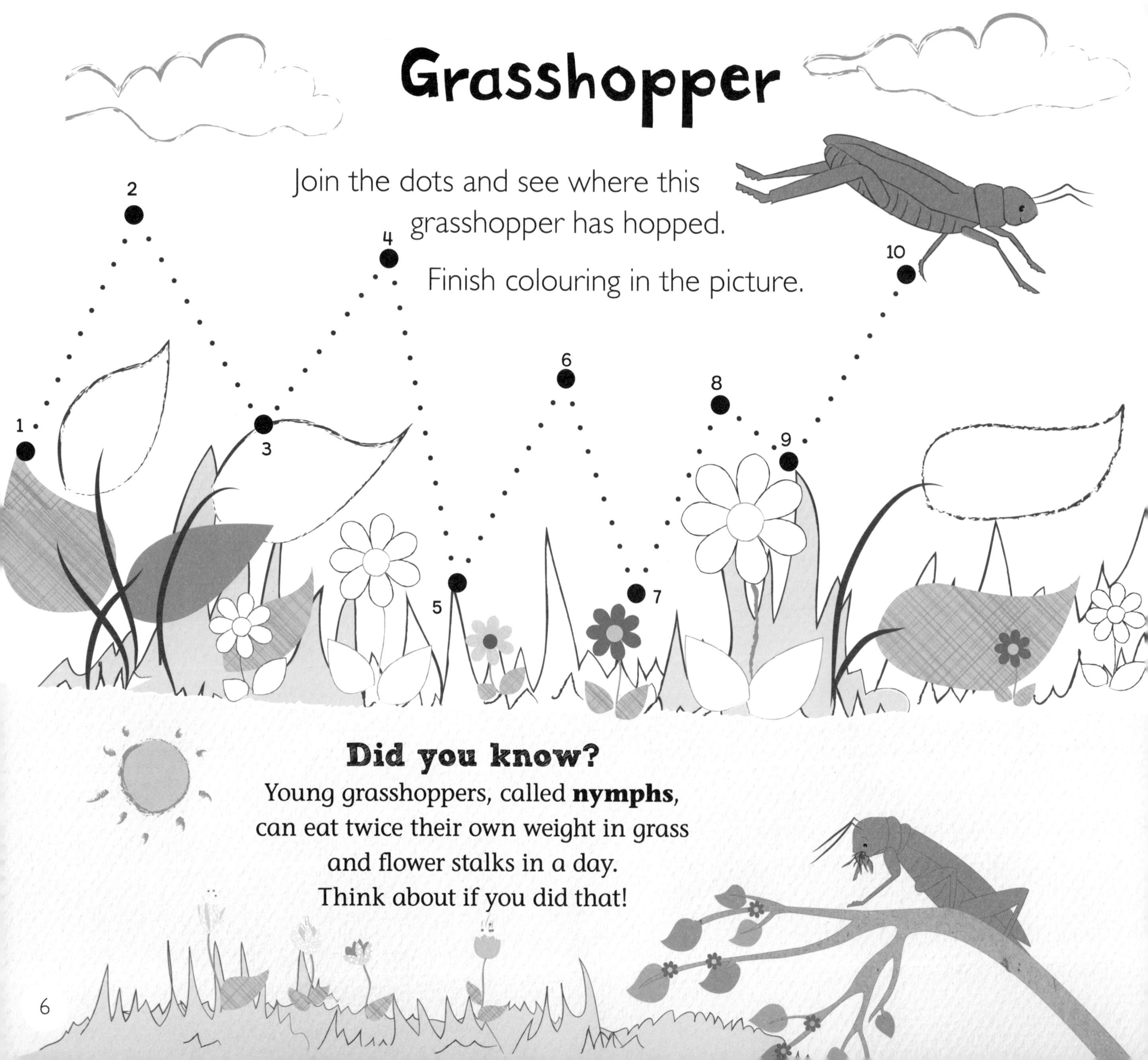

Did you know?

Young grasshoppers, called **nymphs**, can eat twice their own weight in grass and flower stalks in a day. Think about if you did that!

Ladybird

One of these ladybirds only has 7 spots.
Circle it with your crayon.
Finish colouring in the picture.

Did you know?

Ladybirds are **brightly coloured** to tell their **predators**, the birds and spiders that try to eat them, that they taste horrible. Ladybirds can be black with red spots, orange with black spots and white with black spots too.

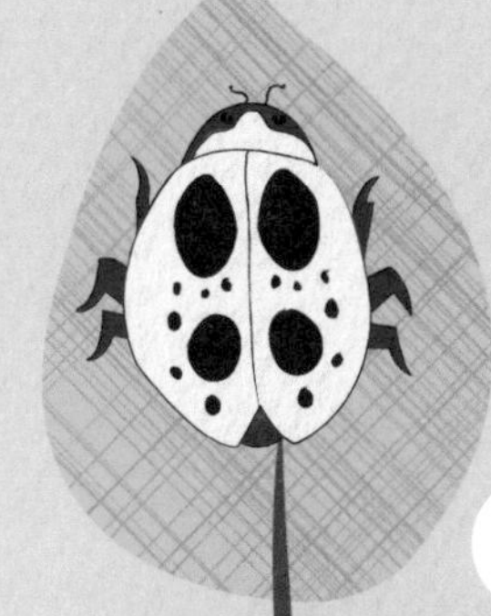

Fly

Flies like to eat rotting food.
Which fly has eaten the rotten apples?

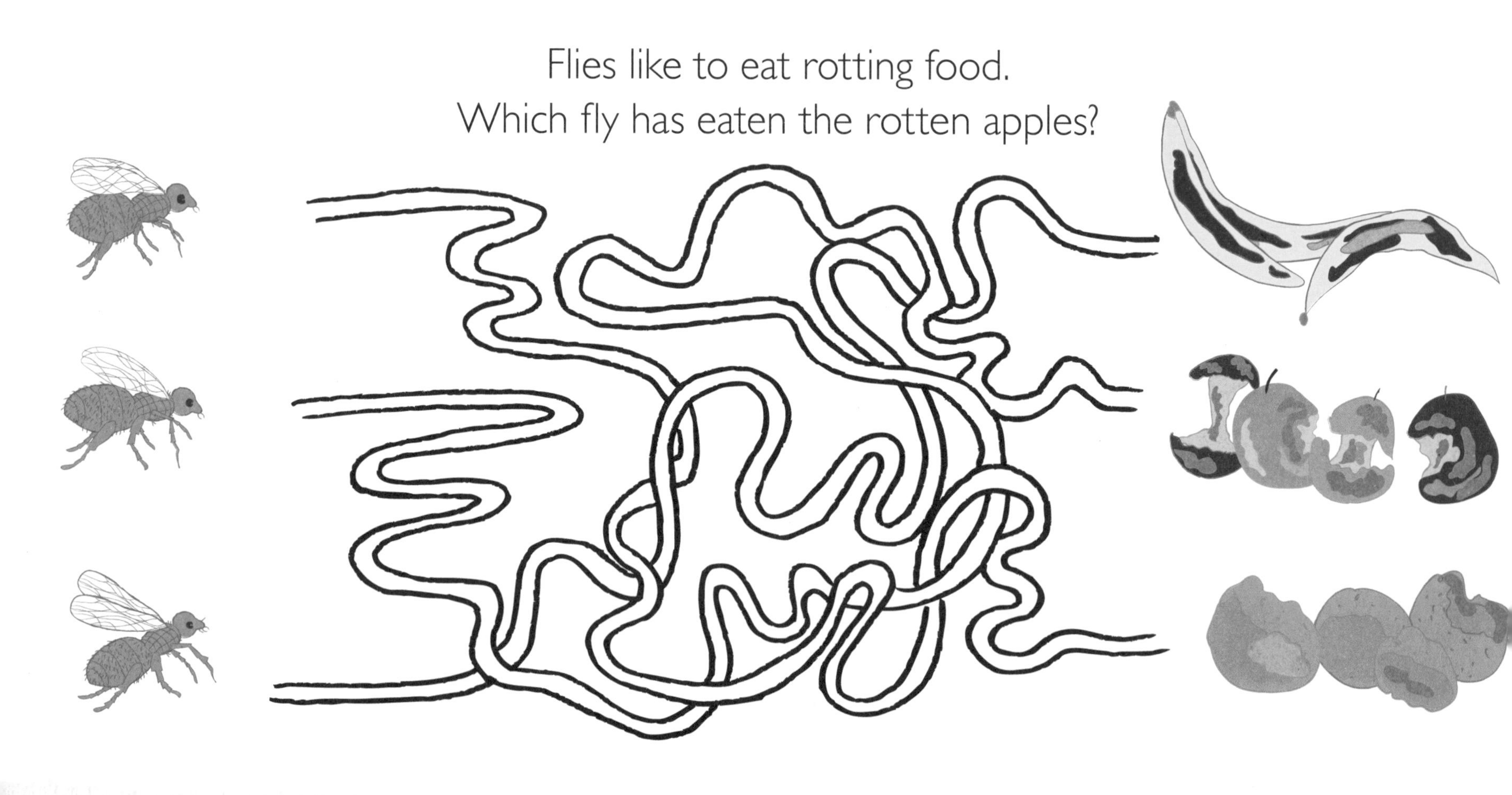

Did you know?

Flies use special **hairs** on their feet to taste what they walk on. If they like the taste then they use their mouths to eat it. They really like eating poo!

Mosquito

Look at this mosquito in the magnifying glass.
Can you spot the mosquito among its friends?

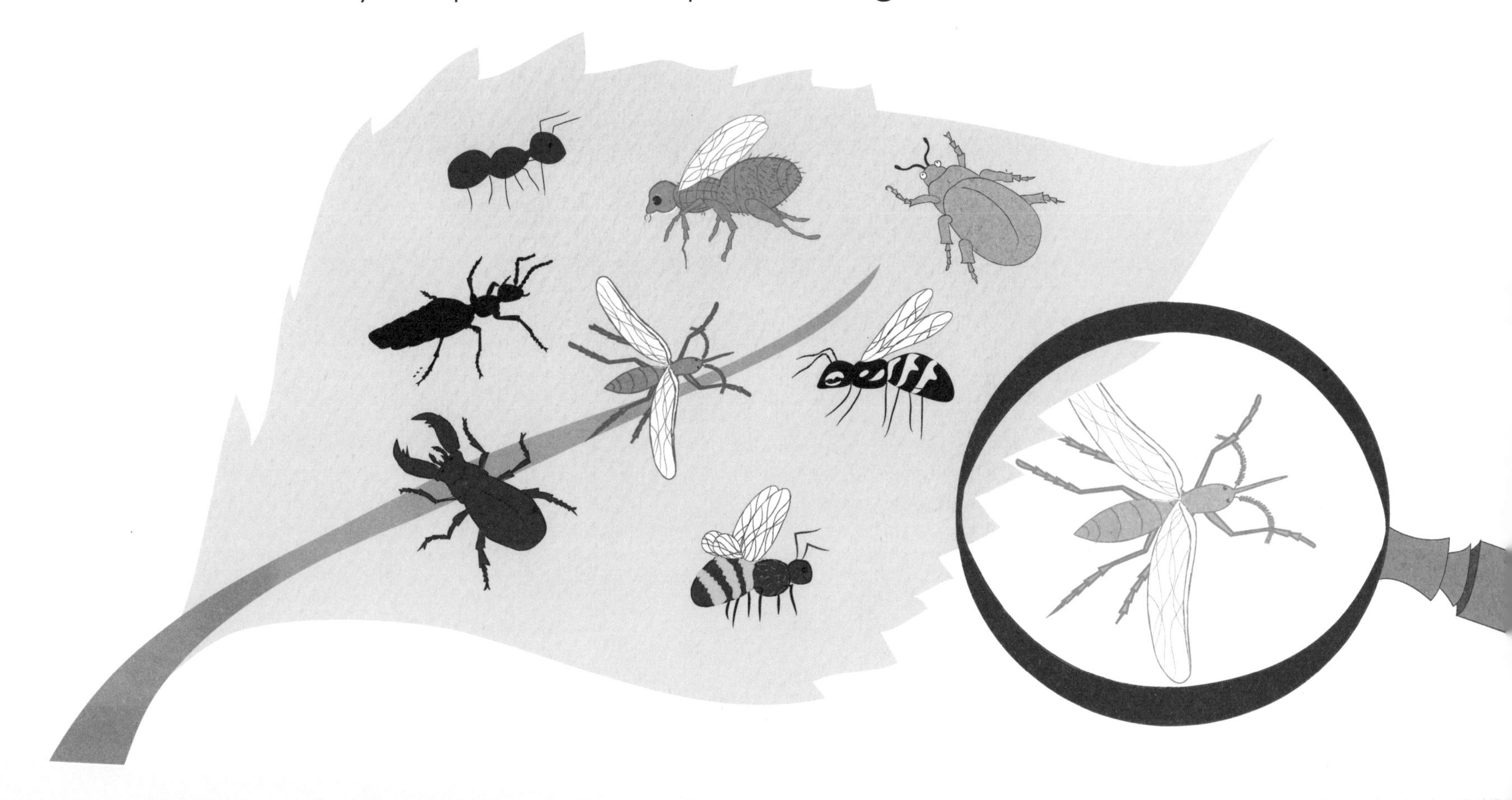

Did you know?

Mosquitoes don't really bite. They **pierce** the skin with their special long sharp 'nose' called a **proboscis** and suck out the blood. Ouch!

Caterpillar

Can you find 3 caterpillars with the same pattern?
Circle them with your crayons.

Did you know?
Caterpillars turn into **moths** or **butterflies.**

Moth

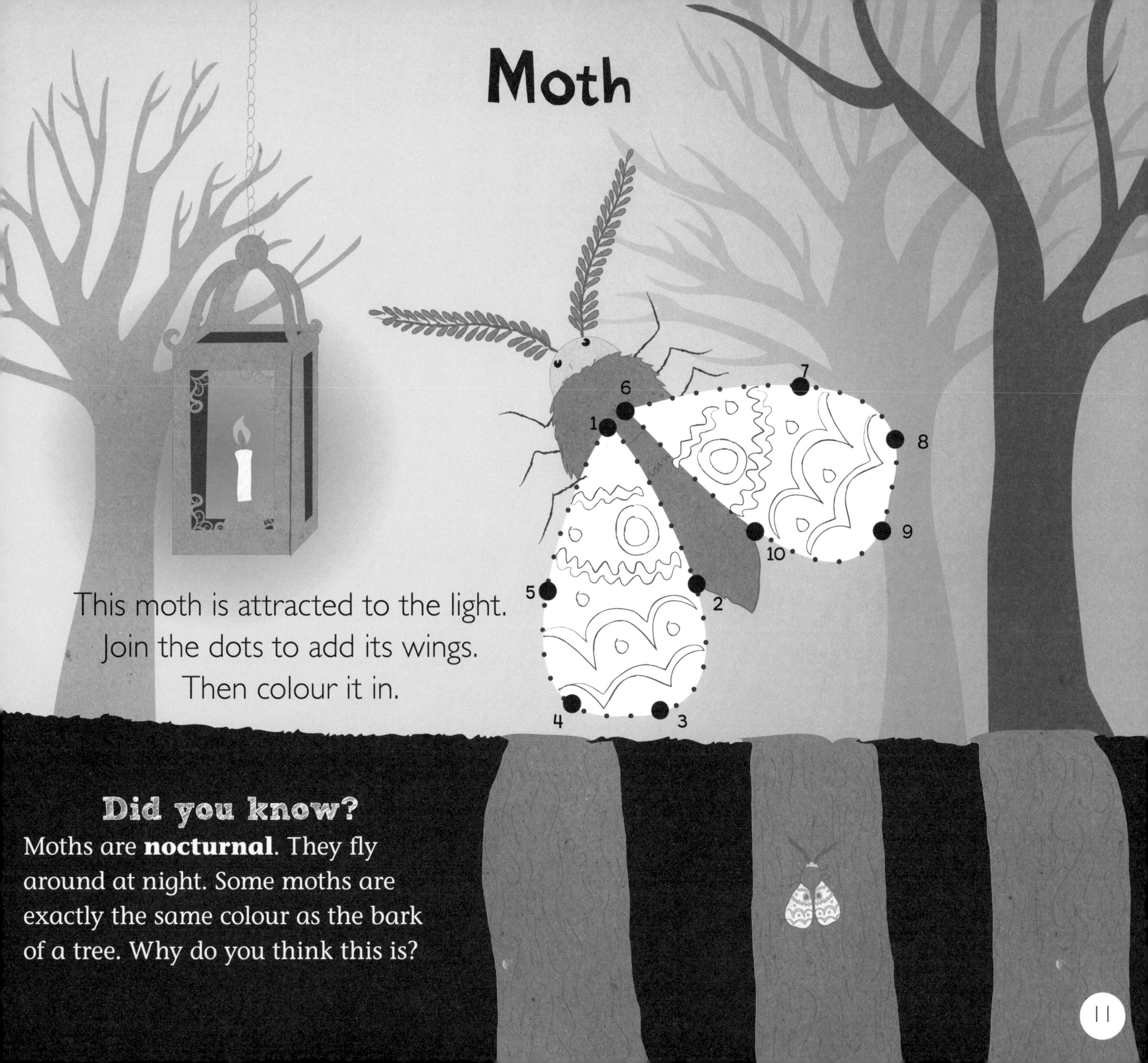

This moth is attracted to the light.
Join the dots to add its wings.
Then colour it in.

Did you know?

Moths are **nocturnal**. They fly around at night. Some moths are exactly the same colour as the bark of a tree. Why do you think this is?

Butterfly

Red Admiral

Cabbage White

Common or Small Blue

Can you find these 3 butterflies in the picture?
Circle them with your crayon.
Finish colouring the picture.

Did you know?
Butterflies start life as **caterpillars**.
Look back at page 10.

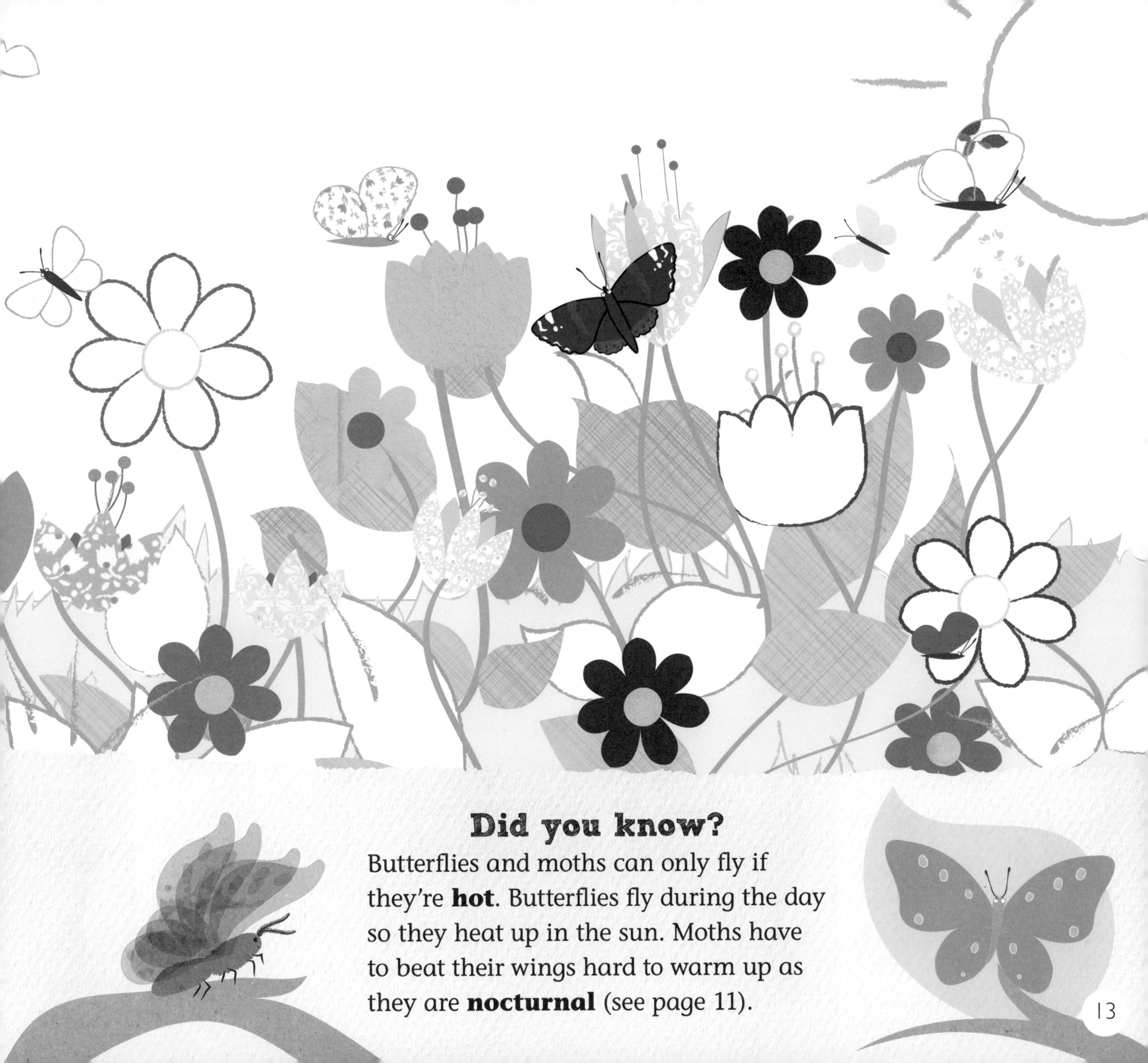

Did you know?

Butterflies and moths can only fly if they're **hot**. Butterflies fly during the day so they heat up in the sun. Moths have to beat their wings hard to warm up as they are **nocturnal** (see page 11).

Ant

This ant lives in a maze of holes,
called an ant colony.
Can you help it find the way out?

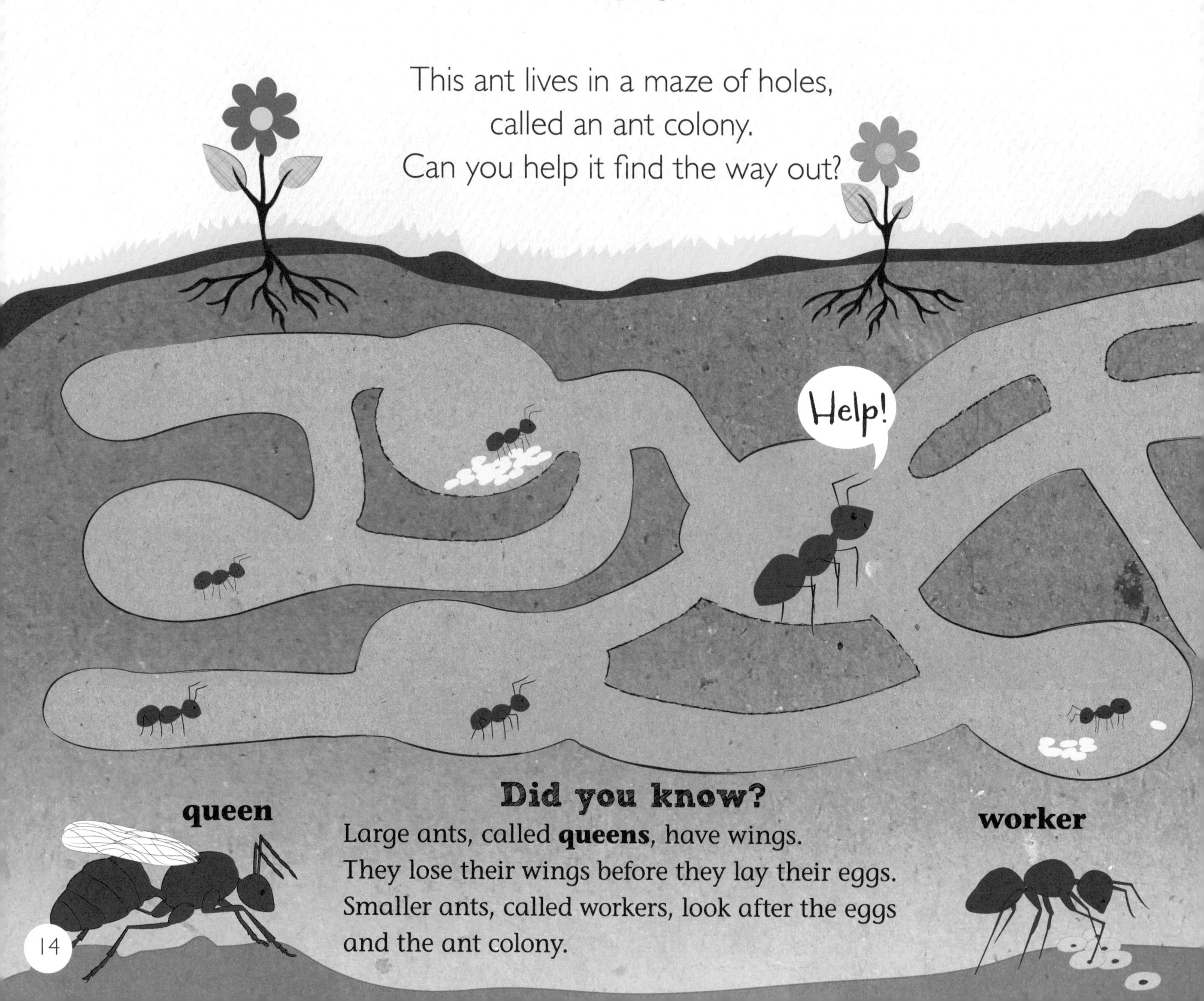

Did you know?

Large ants, called **queens**, have wings.
They lose their wings before they lay their eggs.
Smaller ants, called workers, look after the eggs
and the ant colony.

Did you know?

Ants are very **strong**. If you were as strong as an ant, you could pick up a car!

Spider

How many flies have these spiders caught?
Join the dots to finish the web.

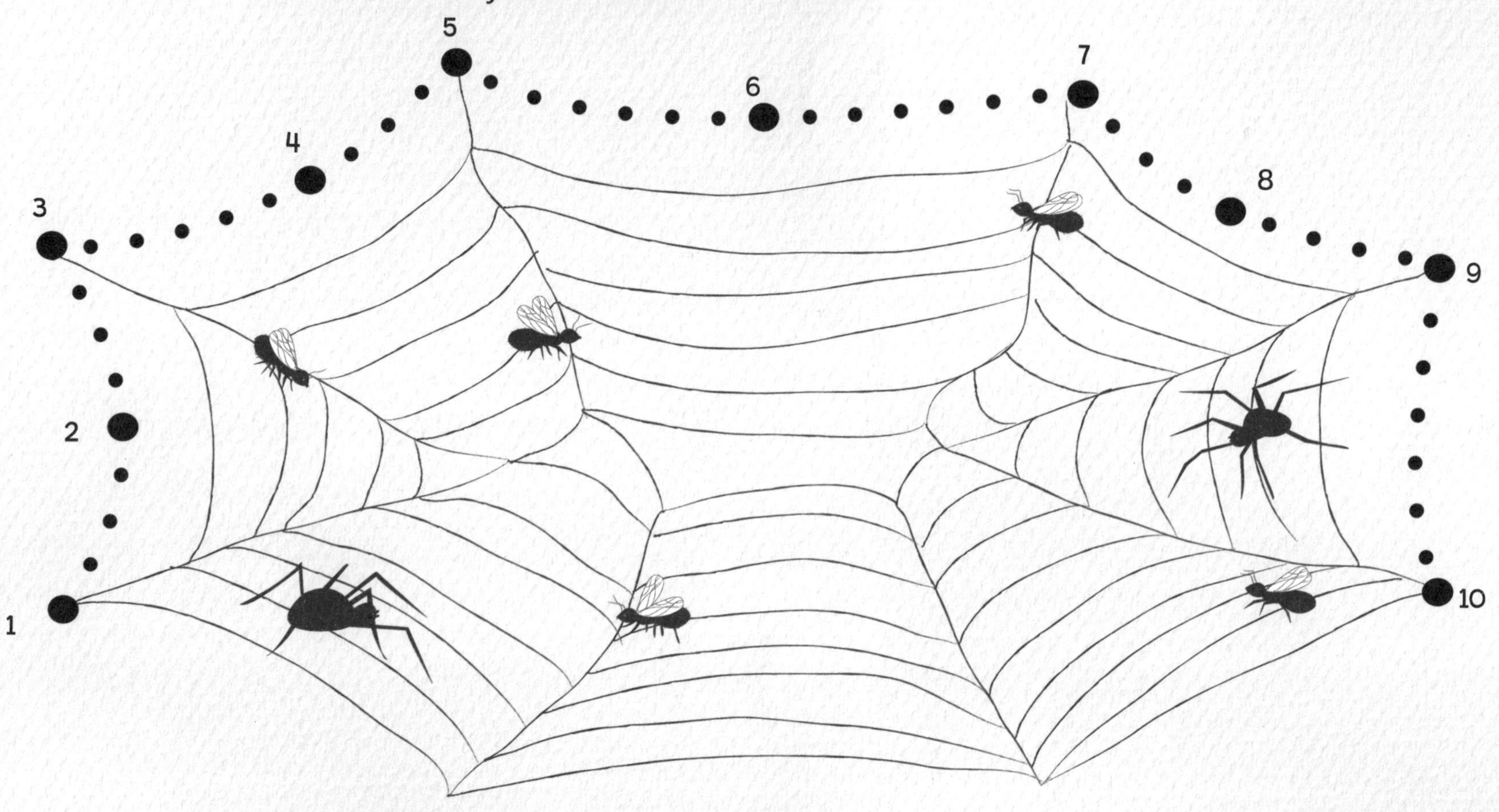

arachnid
(spider)

Did you know?

Spiders aren't insects, they are **arachnids**.
Insects have 6 legs. Arachnids have 8 legs.

insect
(beetle)

Beetle

Each of these beetles has a pair.
Can you match them up?

Did you know?

Beetles chew their food using their special jaws, called **mandibles**. Some beetles have very big mandibles and they also use them for fighting.

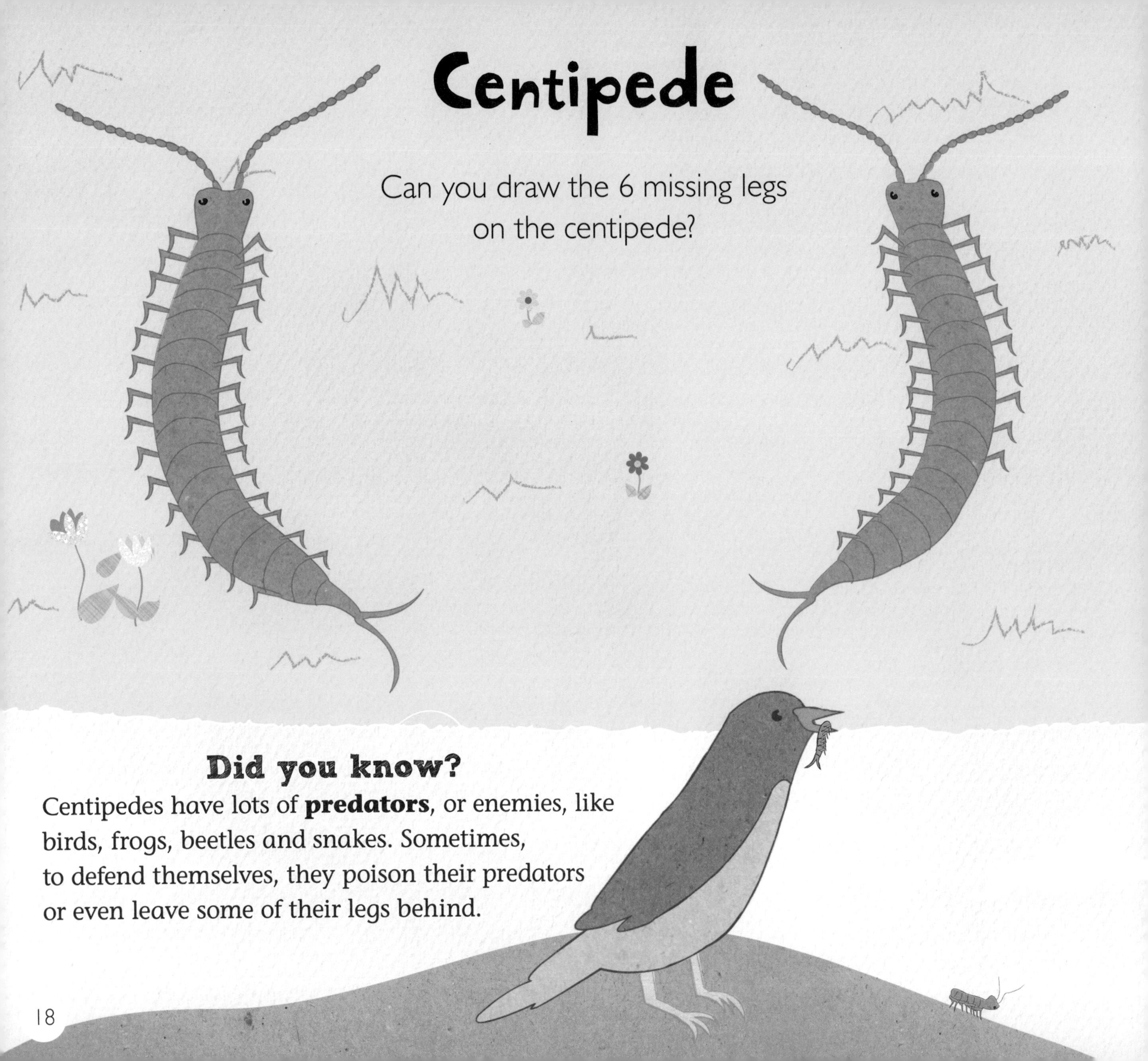

Centipede

Can you draw the 6 missing legs
on the centipede?

Did you know?

Centipedes have lots of **predators**, or enemies, like
birds, frogs, beetles and snakes. Sometimes,
to defend themselves, they poison their predators
or even leave some of their legs behind.

Woodlouse

There are 4 woodlice under this stone.
If you add 2 more, how many will there be?
Write the number here then draw them in.

Did you know?

Toads, spiders and even centipedes **eat woodlice**. They try to defend themselves by curling up into a ball.

Snail

Which of these snails ate the juicy leaves on the wall?

Did you know?

The snail's thick **slime** means that it can crawl over very sharp things, like broken glass, without getting hurt. It can also crawl upside down. (A slug can do this too because it's really a snail without a shell.)

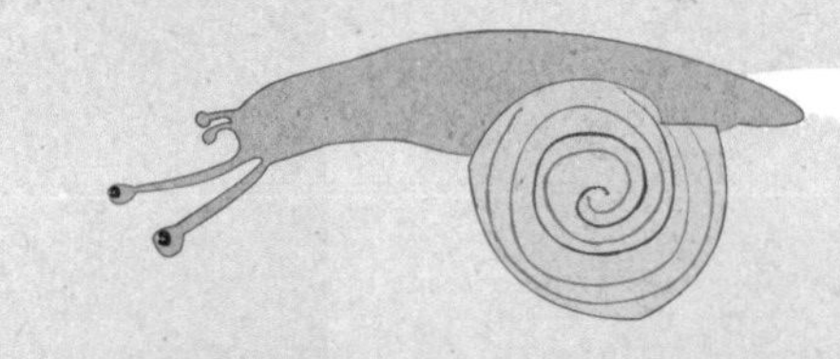

Slug

Can you find 7 slugs in this picture?
Are they all the same colour?

Did you know?

A slug has thousands of **teeth** – more than a shark! It needs them to chew up all those rotting leaves.

Answers

pages 2-3

Can you spot 18 different bugs and butterflies in this picture?
Turn the page to find out more about them...

pages 4-5

Honey Bee
Count the bees on their way to the hive.
10 bees
Did you know?
Bees make honey. Bees must visit about two million flowers to make half a kilo of honey.
Wasp
These wasps want to eat the picnic food. Can you spot 5 differences between the pictures?
Colour in the picnic cloth.
Did you know?
Honey bees die after they sting you. Wasps and bumble bees can pull out their stinger and sting you again. So watch out!

pages 6-7

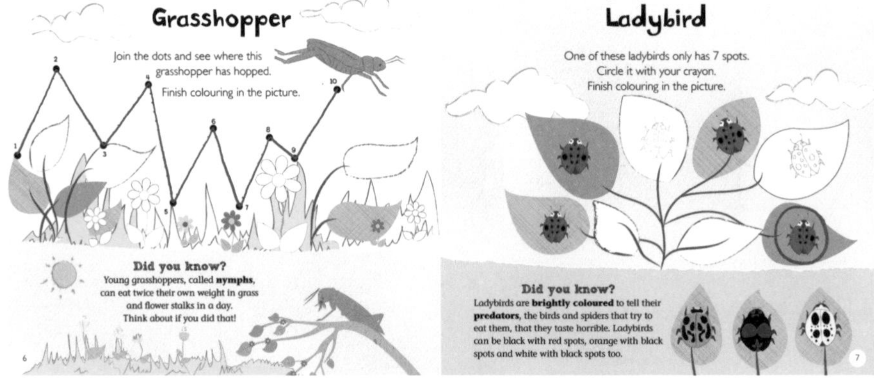

Grasshopper
Join the dots and see where this grasshopper has hopped.
Finish colouring in the picture.
Did you know?
Young grasshoppers, called nymphs, can eat twice their own weight in grass and flower stalks in a day. Think about if you did that!
Ladybird
One of these ladybirds only has 7 spots. Circle it with your crayon. Finish colouring in the picture.
Did you know?
Ladybirds are brightly coloured to tell their predators, the birds and spiders that try to eat them, that they taste horrible. Ladybirds can be black with red spots, orange with black spots and white with black spots too.

pages 8-9

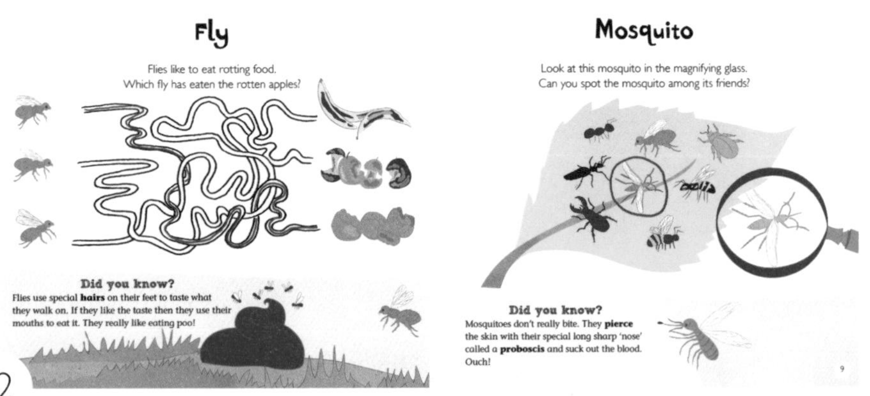

Fly
Flies like to eat rotting food. Which fly has eaten the rotten apples?
Did you know?
Flies use special hairs on their feet to taste what they walk on. If they like the taste then they use their mouths to eat it. They really like eating poo!
Mosquito
Look at this mosquito in the magnifying glass. Can you spot the mosquito among its friends?
Did you know?
Mosquitoes don't really bite. They pierce the skin with their special long sharp 'nose' called a proboscis and suck out the blood. Ouch!

pages 10-11

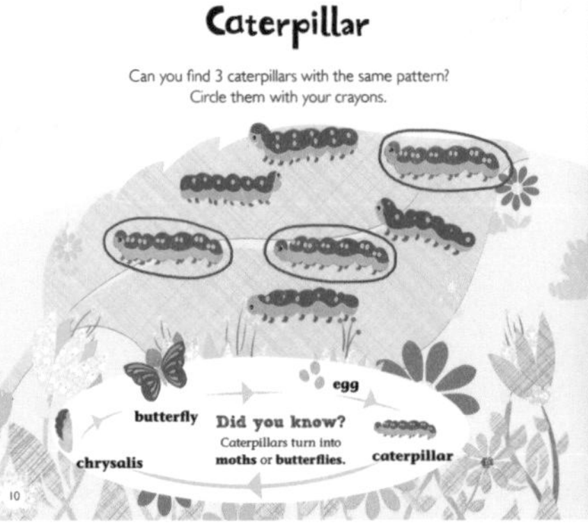

Caterpillar
Can you find 3 caterpillars with the same pattern? Circle them with your crayons.
egg
butterfly
Did you know?
Caterpillars turn into moths or butterflies.
chrysalis
caterpillar

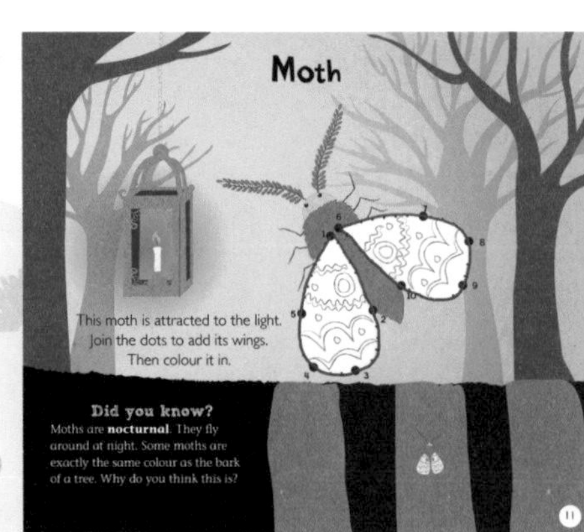

Moth
This moth is attracted to the light. Join the dots to add its wings. Then colour it in.
Did you know?
Moths are nocturnal. They fly around at night. Some moths are exactly the same colour as the bark of a tree. Why do you think this is?

pages 12-13

Butterfly
Can you find these three butterflies in the picture?
Circle them with your crayon.
Finish colouring the picture.
Red Admiral
Cabbage White
Common or Small Blue
Did you know?
Butterflies start life as caterpillars. Look back at page 10.
Did you know?
Butterflies and moths can only fly if they're hot. Butterflies fly during the day so they heat up in the sun. Moths have to beat their wings hard to warm up as they are nocturnal (see page 11).
12
13

pages 14-15

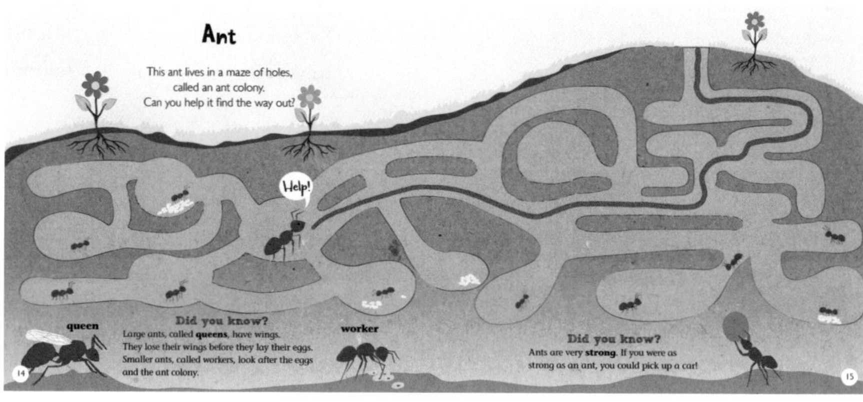
Ant
This ant lives in a maze of holes, called an ant colony.
Can you help it find the way out?
Help!
queen
Did you know?
Large ants, called queens, have wings. They lose their wings before they lay their eggs. Smaller ants, called workers, look after the eggs and the ant colony.
worker
Did you know?
Ants are very strong. If you were as strong as an ant, you could pick up a car!
14
15

pages 16-17

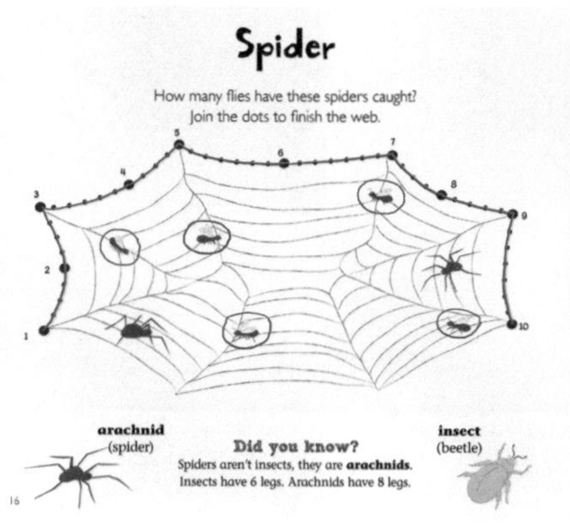
Spider
How many flies have these spiders caught?
Join the dots to finish the web.
arachnid
(spider)
Did you know?
Spiders aren't insects, they are arachnids. Insects have 6 legs. Arachnids have 8 legs.
insect
(beetle)
16

Beetle
Each of these beetles has a pair.
Can you match them up?
Did you know?
Beetles chew their food using their special jaws, called mandibles. Some beetles have very big mandibles and they also use them for fighting.
17

pages 18-19

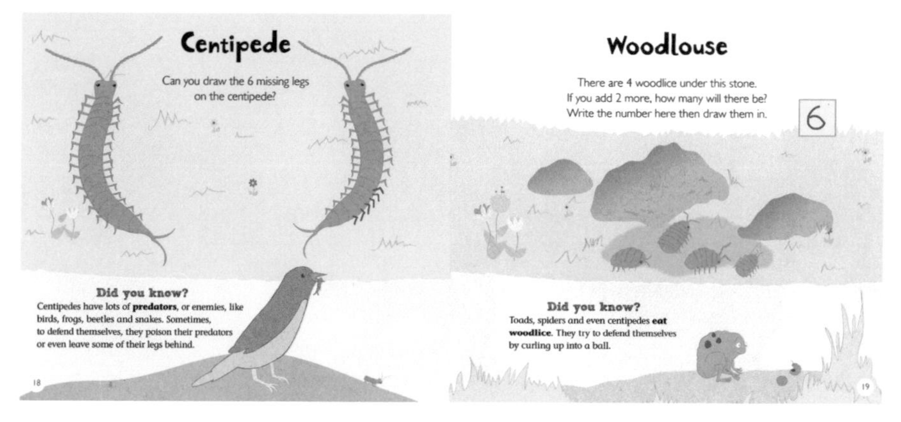
Centipede
Can you draw the 6 missing legs on the centipede?
Did you know?
Centipedes have lots of predators, or enemies, like birds, frogs, beetles and snakes. Sometimes, to defend themselves, they poison their predators or even leave some of their legs behind.
Woodlouse
There are 4 woodlice under this stone.
If you add 2 more, how many will there be?
Write the number here then draw them in.
6
Did you know?
Toads, spiders and even centipedes eat woodlice. They try to defend themselves by curling up into a ball.
18
19

pages 20-21

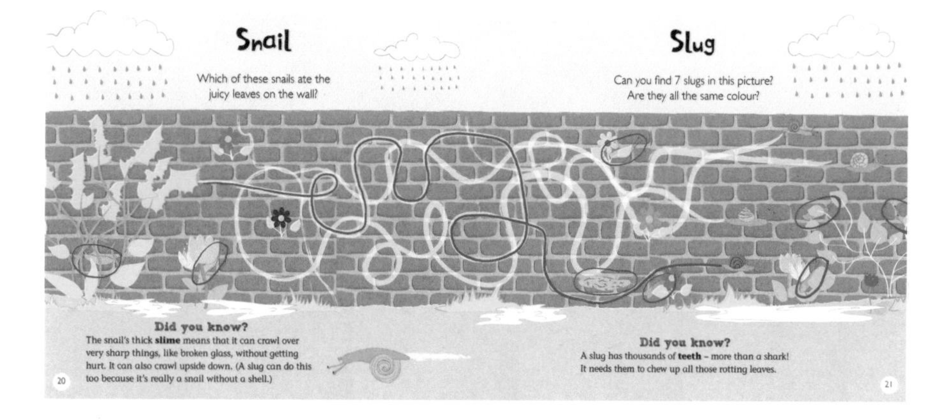
Snail
Which of these snails ate the juicy leaves on the wall?
Slug
Can you find 7 slugs in this picture?
Are they all the same colour?
Did you know?
The snail's thick slime means that it can crawl over very sharp things, like broken glass, without getting hurt. It can also crawl upside down. (A slug can do this too because it's really a snail without a shell.)
Did you know?
A slug has thousands of teeth – more than a shark! It needs them to chew up all those rotting leaves.
20
21

How to Spot Bugs

The activities on these pages will have taught you a bit about bugs and butterflies. Now it's time to put on your best camouflage and get out into the wild. Here are a few bugspotter's tips to help you..

Firstly, think about where you are likely to see bugs and butterflies. This could be in your local park, your garden or your window box. Make sure you get permission from an adult before you decide where to go.

Secondly, wearing appropriate clothes that blend into your surroundings will be good camouflage. You might need binoculars or a magnifying glass and don't forget a packed lunch if you are going to be out all day.

Thirdly, too much noise or movement will scare away all of the bugs and butterflies. So stay very still or move very slowly and carefully. Be patient and wait.

Fourthly, most of the creatures in this book are harmless but some of them, such as wasps and bees, can give you a nasty sting. Be very careful before approaching a creature and make sure you know if it might hurt you or not.

Fifthly, look at what they are doing and see if you can work out why.

Sixthly, using the flashcards in this book, record which bugs and butterflies you have spotted.

Lastly, if you want to learn more about any of the bugs or butterflies, you can do this on the internet or at your local library.

Published by b small publishing ltd.
www.bsmall.co.uk

1 2 3 4 5
ISBN 978-1-909767-41-6
Printed in China by WKT Co. Ltd.

Design: Louise Millar *Editorial:* Sam Hutchinson *Production:* Madeleine Ehm

British Library Cataloguing-in-Publication Data.
A catalogue record for this book is available from the British Library.